TUBERCULOSIS EDUCATION FOR HEALTHCARE CARE PROVIDERS

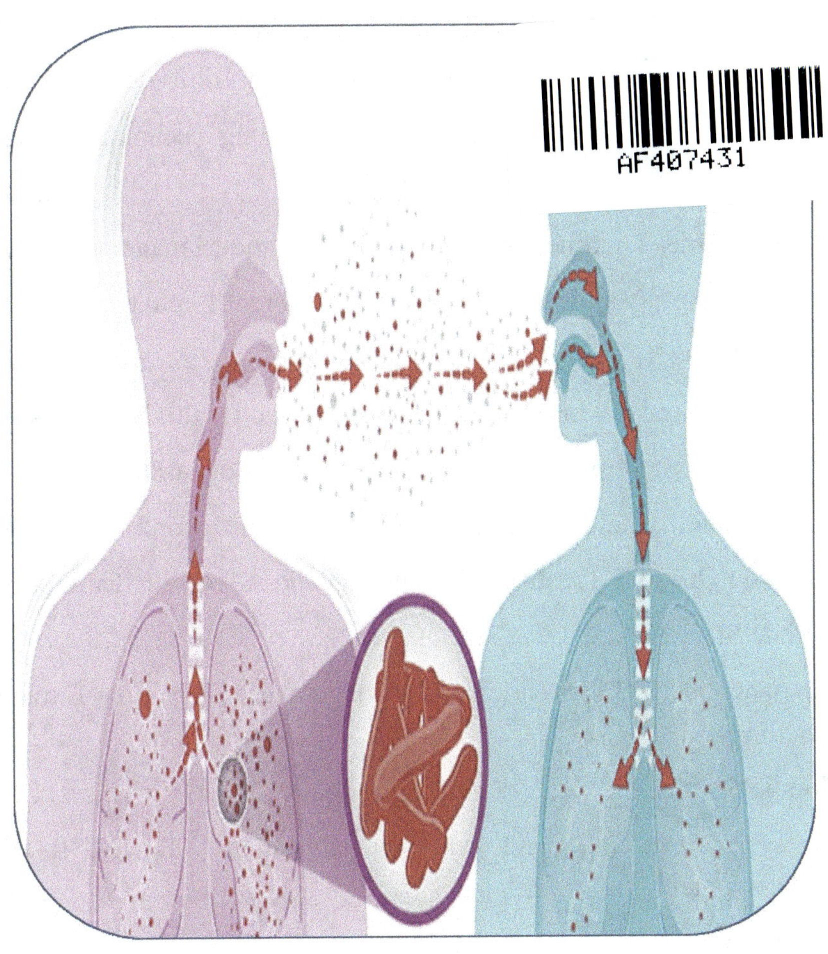

TABLE OF CONTENTS

COURSE OVERVIEW:

This course provides an in-depth exploration of tuberculosis (TB), tailored specifically for healthcare providers, including respiratory therapists, doctors, and nurses. Participants will gain a thorough understanding of TB from its historical context to current challenges and future directions in TB care. The course covers the pathophysiology, clinical presentation, diagnostic methods, and radiological findings associated with TB. It also delves into the pharmacological and non-pharmacological management of the disease, with special attention to TB in unique populations such as children, the elderly, and individuals with HIV/AIDS.

COURSE OBJECTIVES:

By the end of this course, participants will be able to: Understand the Basics of Tuberculosis, Comprehend the Pathophysiology of TB, Identify Clinical and Radiological Signs, mplement Diagnostic and Treatment Strategies, Address TB in Special Populations, Apply Non-Pharmacological Interventions, Engage in Community-Based TB Control, Stay Informed on Research and Innovations, Contribute to Global TB Eradication Efforts, Through this comprehensive course, healthcare providers will be well-prepared to tackle the multifaceted challenges of TB and contribute to its control and eventual eradication.

COURSE MATERIALS

To learn this course, **healthcare providers/ participants** must be provided with materials like a Pen, pencil, notebook, and notepad to better understand and make it easy for them to learn.

INTRODUCTION

Tuberculosis (TB) remains one of the most significant infectious diseases affecting populations worldwide. Despite advances in medical science and healthcare, TB continues to pose substantial challenges to healthcare providers, including respiratory therapists, doctors, and nurses. This comprehensive guide, "Tuberculosis Education for Healthcare Providers: Comprehensive Guide for Respiratory Therapists, Doctors, and Nurses," aims to equip healthcare professionals with the necessary knowledge and skills to effectively diagnose, treat, and manage TB.

TB is caused by the bacterium Mycobacterium tuberculosis. It primarily affects the lungs but can spread to other parts of the body, including the kidneys, spine, and brain. Understanding the epidemiology, clinical manifestations, diagnostic methods, treatment options, and preventive measures is crucial for healthcare providers working in various settings, from hospitals to community health centers. readers will have a comprehensive understanding of TB, from its basic biology to advanced treatment and prevention strategies. The knowledge gained will empower healthcare providers to make informed decisions, provide high-quality care, and contribute to the global effort to eradicate TB. This guide is not only informative but also engaging, designed to inspire and motivate healthcare professionals in their fight against TB.

MODULE ONE

LESSON ONE: INTRODUCTION TO TUBERCULOSIS (TB)

Tuberculosis (TB) is an infectious disease caused by the bacterium Mycobacterium tuberculosis. It primarily affects the lungs but can also involve other organs. TB has been a major health problem for centuries, and despite advancements in medicine, it remains a leading cause of morbidity and mortality worldwide. This lesson provides a comprehensive overview of TB, including its history, global impact, and microbiology.

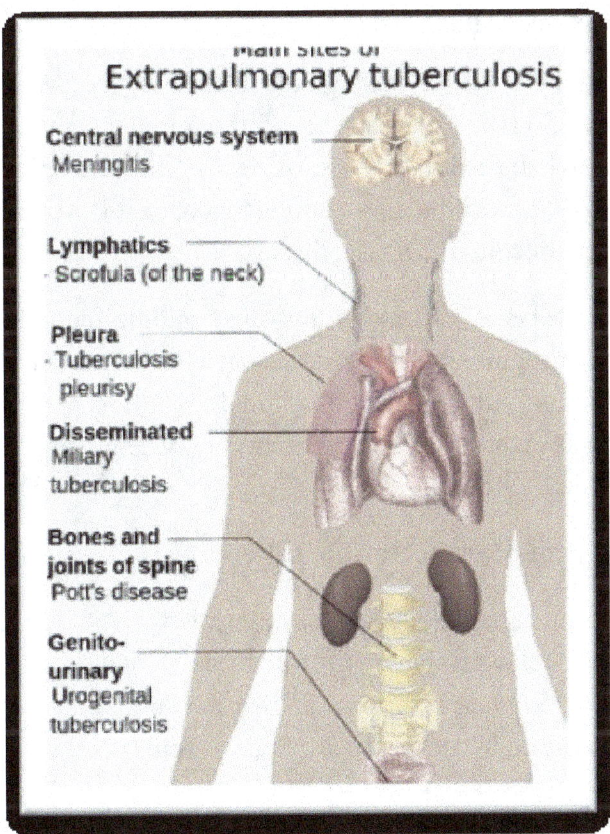

History of Tuberculosis

TB has been present in humans for thousands of years. Evidence of the disease has been found in the spines of Egyptian mummies dating back to 3000-2400 BC. In the 17th and 18th centuries, TB became known as the "White Plague" due to its high mortality rate and widespread prevalence in Europe. The industrial revolution and urbanization contributed to the rapid spread of the disease.

The discovery of the TB bacterium by Robert Koch in 1882 was a significant milestone in understanding and combating the disease. Koch's postulates provided a framework for identifying the causative agents of infectious diseases, and his work laid the foundation for modern microbiology.

Global Impact of Tuberculosis

TB is a global health crisis. According to the World Health Organization (WHO), TB is one of the top ten causes of death worldwide and the leading cause of death from a single infectious agent. In 2019, an estimated 10 million people fell ill with TB, and 1.4 million people died from the disease.

The burden of TB is highest in low- and middle-income countries, particularly in regions with high rates of HIV infection. TB is also prevalent among vulnerable populations, including people living in poverty, those with compromised immune systems, and individuals in overcrowded settings.

Microbiology of Mycobacterium tuberculosis

Mycobacterium tuberculosis is a slow-growing, acid-fast bacterium. It has a unique cell wall rich in mycolic acids, which makes it resistant to many common antibiotics and disinfectants. The bacterium is transmitted through airborne droplets when an infected person coughs, sneezes, or talks.

Once inhaled, M. tuberculosis can evade the host's immune defenses and establish infection in the lungs. The bacteria can remain dormant for years, leading to latent TB infection (LTBI), or they can multiply and cause active TB disease.

Pathogenesis of Tuberculosis

The pathogenesis of TB involves a complex interaction between the bacterium and the host's immune system. Upon inhalation, the bacteria are engulfed by alveolar macrophages in the lungs. M. tuberculosis can survive and replicate within these cells by inhibiting phagosome-lysosome fusion and evading the host's immune response.

The formation of granulomas, or tubercles, is a hallmark of TB infection. Granulomas are organized structures composed of macrophages, T cells, and other immune cells that attempt to contain the infection. In some cases, the bacteria can escape from the granulomas, leading to active TB disease.

Understanding the history, global impact, and microbiology of TB is essential for healthcare providers. This knowledge forms the foundation for diagnosing, treating, and preventing the disease. The following lessons will build on this information, providing detailed insights into the clinical and physiological aspects of TB, as well as practical guidance on its diagnosis and management.

DISCUSSION QUESTIONS

- How do socioeconomic factors influence the global burden of tuberculosis, and what measures can be taken to address these issues?
- Discuss the historical impact of tuberculosis on public health policies and how modern approaches have evolved to tackle the disease.

LESSON TWO: CLINICAL SIGNS AND SYMPTOMS OF TB

Recognizing the clinical signs and symptoms of TB is crucial for early diagnosis and treatment. TB can present with a wide range of symptoms, depending on the site of infection and the patient's immune status. This lesson provides a detailed overview of the clinical manifestations of pulmonary and extrapulmonary TB.

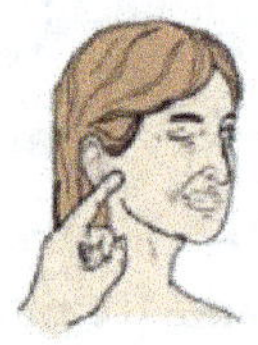
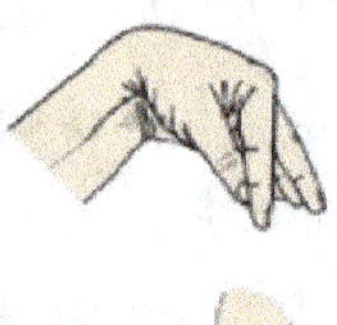
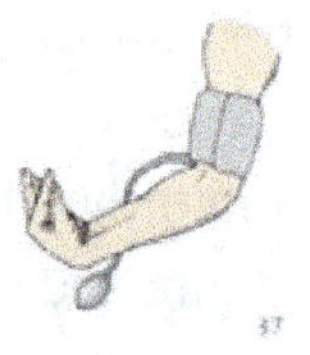

Pulmonary TB

Pulmonary TB is the most common form of the disease, accounting for the majority of TB cases. The primary symptoms of pulmonary TB include:

- Persistent Cough: A cough lasting more than three weeks is a key symptom of TB. It may start as a dry cough and progress to a productive cough with sputum.

- Hemoptysis: Coughing up blood or blood-streaked sputum is a significant indicator of TB.
- Chest Pain: Patients may experience chest pain, particularly when coughing or taking deep breaths.
- Fever: Low-grade fever, often worse in the evening, is a common symptom of TB.
- Night Sweats: Profuse sweating at night, leading to drenched sheets and clothing, is a characteristic symptom.
- Weight Loss: Unintentional weight loss and loss of appetite are common in TB patients.
- Fatigue: Persistent fatigue and weakness can significantly affect the patient's quality of life.

Extrapulmonary TB

Extrapulmonary TB occurs when the infection spreads outside the lungs. It can affect various organs and tissues, leading to a diverse range of symptoms:

- Lymphatic TB: Enlargement of lymph nodes, particularly in the neck (cervical lymphadenitis or scrofula), is a common manifestation.
- Skeletal TB: Involvement of bones and joints, leading to pain, swelling, and restricted movement. Pott's disease (TB of the spine) can cause severe back pain and deformities.
- Genitourinary TB: Symptoms may include dysuria, hematuria, and flank pain. Genital TB can cause pelvic pain and infertility.
- Central Nervous System TB: TB meningitis presents with headache, fever, neck stiffness, and neurological deficits. TB brain abscesses or tuberculomas can cause seizures and focal neurological symptoms.
- Gastrointestinal TB: Abdominal pain, diarrhea, and bowel obstruction are common in TB of the intestines. Hepatic TB can cause jaundice and liver enlargement.

- Miliary TB: A disseminated form of TB characterized by tiny nodules in multiple organs, leading to systemic symptoms such as fever, night sweats, and weight loss.

Differential Diagnosis

The symptoms of TB can overlap with other respiratory and systemic diseases, making differential diagnosis essential. Conditions that can mimic TB include:

- Pneumonia: Bacterial, viral, or fungal pneumonia can present with similar respiratory symptoms.
- Lung Cancer: Persistent cough, hemoptysis, and weight loss can also be seen in lung cancer.
- Chronic Obstructive Pulmonary Disease (COPD): COPD exacerbations can resemble TB symptoms.
- Sarcoidosis: This inflammatory disease can cause granulomas and systemic symptoms similar to TB.
- HIV/AIDS: Co-infection with HIV can complicate the clinical presentation of TB.

Accurate recognition of the clinical signs and symptoms of TB is critical for timely diagnosis and treatment. Healthcare providers must maintain a high index of suspicion for TB, especially in high-risk populations and areas with a high prevalence of the disease. The next lesson will delve into the physiological signs and pathophysiology of TB, providing a deeper understanding of the disease process.

DISCUSSION QUESTIONS

- How does Mycobacterium tuberculosis evade the host immune system, and what implications does this have for developing effective treatments?
- Compare and contrast the immune responses in latent TB infection versus active TB disease. What factors contribute to the transition from latency to active disease?

MODULE TWO

LESSON ONE; PHYSIOLOGICAL SIGNS AND PATHOPHYSIOLOGY OF TB

Understanding the physiological signs and pathophysiology of TB is essential for comprehending how the disease affects the body and for guiding appropriate treatment. This lesson explores the mechanisms of TB infection, the body's immune response, and the physiological changes that occur during the disease.

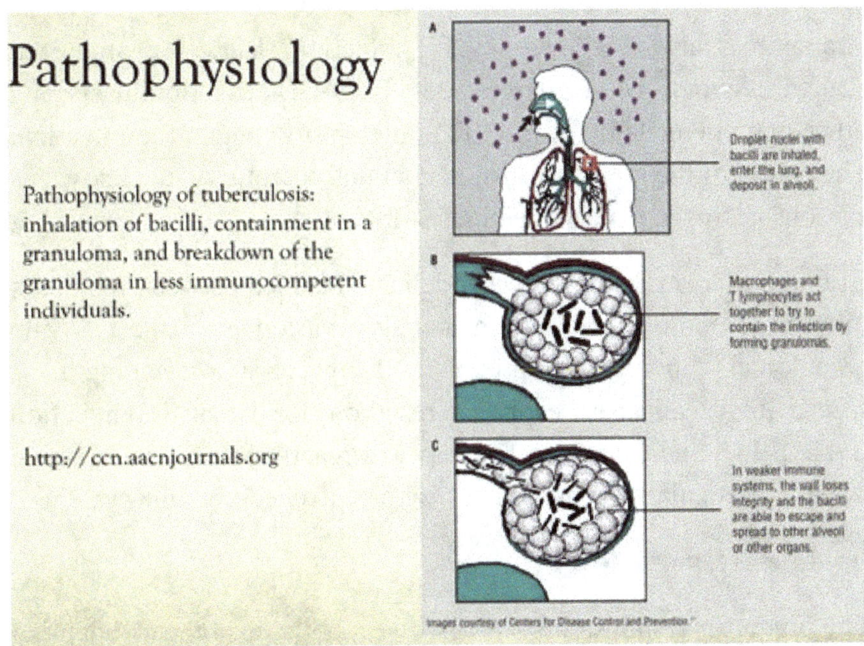

Pathophysiology

Pathophysiology of tuberculosis: inhalation of bacilli, containment in a granuloma, and breakdown of the granuloma in less immunocompetent individuals.

http://ccn.aacnjournals.org

Mechanisms of TB Infection

The initial step in TB infection is the inhalation of airborne droplets containing Mycobacterium tuberculosis. Once inhaled, the bacteria reach the alveoli in the lungs, where they are engulfed by alveolar macrophages. M. tuberculosis has evolved various mechanisms to survive and replicate within these macrophages, including:

- Inhibition of Phagosome-Lysosome Fusion: M. tuberculosis prevents the fusion of phagosomes with lysosomes, avoiding the acidic and enzymatic environment that would normally kill the bacteria.
- Resistance to Reactive Oxygen and Nitrogen Species: The bacterium possesses enzymes that neutralize reactive oxygen and nitrogen species produced by the host's immune cells.
- Modulation of Host Immune Response: M. tuberculosis can manipulate the host's immune response to create a more favorable environment for its survival and replication.

Granuloma Formation

Granulomas are a hallmark of TB infection. These are organized structures composed of macrophages, T cells, B cells, fibroblasts, and other immune cells that form in an attempt to contain the infection. The center of the granuloma often contains necrotic tissue, known as caseous necrosis, which resembles soft cheese.

Granuloma formation involves a delicate balance between the host's immune response and the bacteria's evasion strategies. While granulomas can effectively contain the bacteria, preventing their spread, they can also become a reservoir for latent TB infection (LTBI). In some cases, the bacteria can reactivate and cause active disease, particularly in individuals with weakened immune systems.

Immune Response to TB

The immune response to TB involves both innate and adaptive immunity. Key components of the immune response include:

- Macrophages: These cells are the primary hosts for M. tuberculosis. They attempt to kill the bacteria through phagocytosis and the production of reactive oxygen and nitrogen species.

- T Cells: CD4+ T cells, particularly Th1 cells, play a crucial role in activating macrophages and enhancing their bactericidal activity. CD8+ T cells can also directly kill infected cells.
- Cytokines: Various cytokines, such as interferon-gamma (IFN-γ) and tumor necrosis factor-alpha (TNF-α), are critical for the containment of TB. These signaling molecules help coordinate the immune response and promote granuloma formation.

Physiological Changes in TB

TB can cause significant physiological changes, particularly in the lungs. These changes include:

- Pulmonary Infiltrates: The accumulation of immune cells and fluid in the lungs can lead to the formation of infiltrates, which are visible on chest X-rays.
- Cavitation: In some cases, the necrotic center of a granuloma can liquefy, leading to the formation of cavities in the lungs. These cavities can harbor large numbers of bacteria and are associated with more severe disease.
- Fibrosis: Chronic inflammation can result in the deposition of fibrous tissue, leading to scarring and reduced lung function.
- Bronchiectasis: Damage to the bronchial walls can cause bronchiectasis, a condition characterized by the abnormal dilation and scarring of the airways.

A thorough understanding of the physiological signs and pathophysiology of TB is essential for healthcare providers. This knowledge not only aids in diagnosing and treating the disease but also provides insights into the mechanisms of immune evasion and persistence used by M. tuberculosis. The following lesson will focus on diagnostic techniques, including the use of X-ray and other imaging modalities, to identify TB and assess the extent of disease involvement.

- Discuss the challenges in diagnosing extrapulmonary TB compared to pulmonary TB. How can healthcare providers improve the accuracy of diagnosis in these cases?
- Evaluate the roles of different diagnostic tests (TST, IGRAs, sputum microscopy, and NAATs) in the context of TB. Which tests are most effective in various clinical scenarios?

LESSON TWO; TB DIAGNOSIS: X-RAY AND IMAGING TECHNIQUES

Accurate diagnosis of TB is critical for effective treatment and control of the disease. Imaging techniques, particularly chest X-rays, play a vital role in the diagnosis and management of TB. This lesson provides a detailed overview of the imaging modalities used in TB diagnosis, including their advantages, limitations, and interpretation.

CHEST X-RAY

Chest radiography is another option for screening, it can be used together with symptom screening to best determine who should continue on with diagnostic testing

Advantages
- Quick
- High sensitivity
- Inexpensive
- Widely used

Disadvantages
- Low specificity
- Requires additional testing
- Cannot be used for extrapulmonary TB
- Active TB doesn't always look the same (especially in people with HIV)

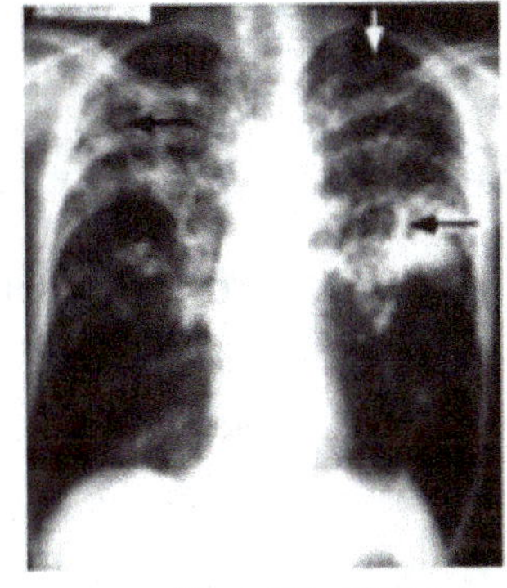

Abnormal Chest X-Ray

Adapted from Dr. Madhukar Pai

Chest X-ray in TB Diagnosis

Chest X-ray is the most commonly used imaging technique for diagnosing pulmonary TB. It provides valuable information about the presence and extent of lung involvement. Key radiographic features of TB include:

- Infiltrates: Patchy or nodular opacities, often located in the upper lobes of the lungs, are common in TB.

- Cavitation: The presence of cavities, particularly in the upper lobes, is highly suggestive of active TB.
- Pleural Effusion: Accumulation of fluid in the pleural space can occur in TB, leading to blunting of the costophrenic angles on X-ray.
- Hilar and Mediastinal Lymphadenopathy: Enlargement of lymph nodes in the hilum and mediastinum is a common finding, particularly in primary TB.
- Fibrosis and Scarring: Chronic TB can result in fibrotic changes and scarring, leading to volume loss and architectural distortion of the lungs.

Limitations of Chest X-ray

While chest X-ray is a valuable tool, it has several limitations:

- Sensitivity and Specificity: X-ray findings can be nonspecific and may overlap with other pulmonary conditions, such as pneumonia, lung cancer, and sarcoidosis.
- Latent TB: Chest X-rays cannot detect latent TB infection (LTBI), as there are no active lesions or abnormalities in the lungs.
- Early Disease: In the early stages of TB, radiographic findings may be subtle or absent, leading to potential false-negative results.
- Extrapulmonary TB: Chest X-rays are limited in diagnosing extrapulmonary TB, as the disease can involve organs outside the thoracic cavity.

Advanced Imaging Techniques

In addition to chest X-rays, several advanced imaging modalities can aid in the diagnosis and assessment of TB:

- Computed Tomography (CT): CT scans provide more detailed images of the lungs and other organs. They are particularly useful for detecting small nodules, cavitations, and mediastinal lymphadenopathy. CT is also valuable in evaluating the extent of disease and guiding biopsy procedures.

- Magnetic Resonance Imaging (MRI): MRI is useful for assessing TB in organs such as the brain, spine, and soft tissues. It provides excellent contrast resolution and can detect inflammation, abscesses, and other abnormalities.
- Ultrasound: Ultrasound is a non-invasive technique that can be used to evaluate pleural effusions, abdominal TB, and lymphadenopathy. It is particularly useful in resource-limited settings due to its portability and affordability.
- Positron Emission Tomography (PET): PET scans, often combined with CT (PET/CT), can assess metabolic activity in TB lesions. They are useful for distinguishing active disease from scar tissue and for evaluating treatment response.

Interpretation of Imaging Findings

Interpreting imaging findings in TB requires a thorough understanding of the disease's radiographic patterns and the ability to correlate these findings with clinical and laboratory data. Key considerations include:

- Clinical Context: Imaging findings should be interpreted in the context of the patient's symptoms, history, and risk factors for TB.
- Comparison with Previous Studies: Comparing current imaging studies with previous ones can help assess disease progression or response to treatment.
- Correlation with Microbiological Results: Imaging findings should be correlated with microbiological tests, such as sputum smear microscopy, culture, and molecular assays, to confirm the diagnosis.

Imaging techniques, particularly chest X-rays, are essential tools in the diagnosis and management of TB. While they have limitations, advances in imaging technology and interpretation can significantly enhance the accuracy and reliability of TB diagnosis. The following lesson will focus on the treatment of TB, detailing the medications used, their mechanisms of action, and the management of drug-resistant TB.

DISCUSSION QUESTIONS

- How can radiological findings guide the differentiation between active TB and other pulmonary diseases? Provide examples of radiographic features specific to TB.
- Discuss the limitations of chest X-rays in diagnosing TB and the advantages of using CT scans and other advanced imaging techniques.

MODULE THREE

LESSON ONE: TREATMENT OF TB: MEDICATION AND MANAGEMENT

Effective treatment of TB involves a combination of medications and careful management to ensure successful outcomes and prevent the development of drug resistance. This lesson provides a comprehensive overview of TB treatment, including first-line and second-line medications, treatment regimens, and the management of drug-resistant TB.

TREATMENT OF TUBERCULOSIS:

Prevention:

- *BCG vaccination:* It does not prevent infection but limits multiplication and spread of following infection so prevents fulminating forms as miliary tuberculosis and tuberculous meningitis. (In Egypt, it is compulsory given to infants in the first 30 days of life subcutaneously in the left deltoid region and a booster dose is given at school age).

- *Chemoprophylaxis:* It is the administration of isoniazide to prevent the development of TB in contacts or susceptible persons (AIDS and immunosuppressed patients) till the original case is considered noninfectious for a maximum of 1 yr.

First-Line Medications for TB

The standard treatment for drug-susceptible TB involves a combination of first-line medications. These include:

- Isoniazid (INH): Isoniazid is a bactericidal drug that inhibits the synthesis of mycolic acids, essential components of the mycobacterial cell wall. It is highly effective against actively dividing TB bacteria.

- Rifampicin (RIF): Rifampicin is a potent bactericidal drug that inhibits RNA synthesis by binding to the bacterial DNA-dependent RNA polymerase. It is effective against both actively dividing and dormant TB bacteria.

- Ethambutol (EMB): Ethambutol is a bacteriostatic drug that inhibits cell wall synthesis by interfering with the synthesis of arabinogalactan. It is used to prevent the development of resistance to other first-line drugs.

- Pyrazinamide (PZA): Pyrazinamide is a prodrug that is converted to its active form, pyrazinoic acid, in the acidic environment of the macrophage phagosome. It is effective against dormant TB bacteria residing within granulomas.

Standard Treatment

Regimens

The World Health Organization (WHO) recommends several standard treatment regimens for drug-susceptible TB, depending on factors such as the patient's age, previous TB treatment history, and the local prevalence of drug resistance. Common regimens include:

- Standard Short-Course Therapy (6 months): This regimen consists of an initial phase of INH, RIF, EMB, and PZA for two months, followed by a continuation phase of INH and RIF for four months.

- Fixed-Dose Combination Therapy: Fixed-dose combinations (FDCs) simplify treatment by combining multiple medications into a single tablet. FDCs improve adherence and reduce the risk of medication errors.

Management of Drug-Resistant TB

Drug-resistant TB is a growing concern due to the emergence of multidrug-resistant (MDR) and extensively drug-resistant (XDR) strains. Treatment of drug-resistant TB requires specialized regimens that include second-line medications, such as:

- Fluoroquinolones: Drugs like levofloxacin and moxifloxacin inhibit DNA gyrase, an enzyme essential for bacterial DNA replication. They are active against many MDR-TB strains.
- Injectable Agents: Drugs like kanamycin, amikacin, and capreomycin inhibit protein synthesis in TB bacteria. They are used in combination with other second-line drugs for MDR-TB treatment.
- Bedaquiline and Linezolid: Bedaquiline targets ATP synthase in TB bacteria, while linezolid inhibits protein synthesis. Both drugs are reserved for XDR-TB and cases of treatment failure with other medications.

Adverse Effects and Monitoring

TB medications can cause a range of adverse effects, including hepatotoxicity, peripheral neuropathy, gastrointestinal disturbances, and QT interval prolongation. Healthcare providers must monitor patients regularly for these adverse effects and adjust treatment regimens as needed.

Treatment Adherence and Support

Ensuring treatment adherence is crucial for successful TB treatment outcomes. Healthcare providers play a vital role in educating patients about the importance of completing their medication courses, monitoring treatment compliance, and addressing barriers to adherence, such as medication side effects and social determinants of health.

Effective treatment of TB requires a multidisciplinary approach, involving healthcare providers, public health officials, and community stakeholders. By understanding the mechanisms of action of TB medications, adhering to treatment guidelines, and monitoring patients closely, healthcare providers can achieve successful treatment outcomes and contribute to global efforts to eliminate TB. The following lesson will explore the manifestations of TB in different populations, highlighting the unique challenges and considerations in TB diagnosis and management.

DISCUSSION QUESTIONS

- What are the key challenges in ensuring adherence to TB treatment regimens, and how can healthcare systems address these challenges?
- Compare the treatment approaches for drug-susceptible TB and multidrug-resistant TB (MDR-TB). What are the main differences in terms of drug selection and treatment duration?

LESSON TWO: MANIFESTATIONS OF TB IN DIFFERENT POPULATIONS

TB can affect individuals of all ages and backgrounds, but certain populations may be at higher risk or face unique challenges in diagnosis and treatment. This lesson explores the manifestations of TB in different populations, including children, elderly individuals, immunocompromised patients, and those with comorbidities.

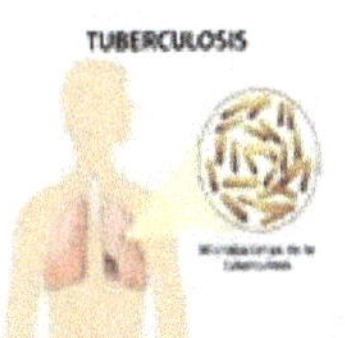

Tuberculosis

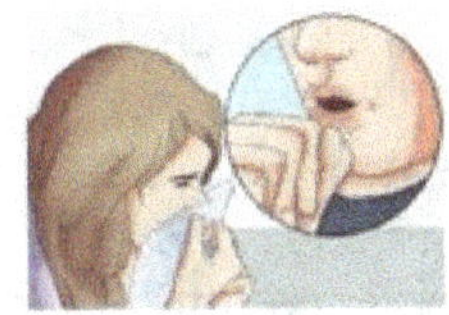

TB in Children

TB in children presents unique challenges due to nonspecific symptoms, difficulty in obtaining sputum samples, and the risk of disseminated disease. Pediatric TB can manifest as:

- Primary TB Complex: Characterized by hilar and mediastinal lymphadenopathy, consolidation, and pleural effusion on chest X-ray.
- Miliary TB: Disseminated disease with multiple small nodules throughout the lungs and extrapulmonary organs. Miliary TB can lead to systemic symptoms such as fever, weight loss, and failure to thrive.

- TB Meningitis: A severe form of extrapulmonary TB that can cause headache, altered mental status, seizures, and focal neurological deficits. Early diagnosis and prompt treatment are critical to prevent neurological sequelae.

TB in Elderly Individuals

Elderly individuals are at increased risk of TB due to age-related immune senescence and the presence of comorbidities such as diabetes mellitus and chronic obstructive pulmonary disease (COPD). TB in the elderly may present with atypical symptoms, such as confusion, falls, anorexia, and functional decline. Delayed diagnosis and treatment can lead to severe disease and poor outcomes.

TB in Immunocompromised Patients

Immunocompromised patients, including those living with HIV/AIDS or receiving immunosuppressive therapy, are at heightened risk of developing TB. HIV infection is the most potent risk factor for TB reactivation and progression from latent TB infection to active disease. TB in immunocompromised patients can present with atypical symptoms and involve multiple organ systems, requiring a high index of suspicion and comprehensive diagnostic evaluation.

TB in Patients with Comorbidities

Patients with comorbidities such as diabetes mellitus, chronic kidney disease, and malignancies are at increased risk of developing TB due to impaired immune function and disease-related complications. TB can exacerbate existing comorbidities and lead to poor treatment outcomes if not promptly diagnosed and managed.

Social Determinants of Health

Social determinants of health, including poverty, homelessness, overcrowded living conditions, and limited access to healthcare services, significantly impact TB incidence and outcomes.

Addressing these social factors is essential for effective TB prevention and control efforts, as well as ensuring equitable access to diagnosis and treatment for all populations.

TB manifests differently in various populations, requiring healthcare providers to adapt their diagnostic and treatment approaches accordingly. By recognizing the unique challenges faced by children, elderly individuals, immunocompromised patients, and those with comorbidities, healthcare providers can improve early detection, enhance treatment outcomes, and reduce TB-related morbidity and mortality. The next lesson will explore preventive measures and public health strategies aimed at controlling the spread of TB and reducing its global burden.

DISCUSSION QUESTIONS

- How do public health interventions such as vaccination, education, and infection control measures contribute to TB prevention and control?
- Discuss the role of nutritional support and socioeconomic interventions in the management of TB patients. How do these non-pharmacological measures impact treatment outcomes?

MODULE FOUR

LESSON ONE: PREVENTIVE MEASURES AND PUBLIC HEALTH STRATEGIES

Preventing the spread of TB and reducing its global burden require a multifaceted approach that includes preventive measures, public health strategies, and community engagement. This lesson explores various strategies aimed at TB prevention, including vaccination, infection control measures, contact tracing, and health education initiatives.

Bacille Calmette-Guérin (BCG) Vaccine

The BCG vaccine is a live attenuated vaccine derived from Mycobacterium bovis and provides partial protection against severe forms of TB, such as TB meningitis and miliary TB, in children. BCG vaccination is recommended for infants and children living in areas with a high prevalence of TB or those at increased risk of exposure to TB.

Infection Control Measures

In healthcare settings, implementing infection control measures is crucial for preventing the transmission of TB to patients, healthcare workers, and visitors. Key infection control practices include:

- Controls: Policies and procedures for TB screening, diagnosis, and treatment, as well as Administrative protocols for managing TB patients in isolation rooms.
- Environmental Controls: Ventilation systems that minimize the concentration of airborne infectious particles, such as negative-pressure isolation rooms and ultraviolet germicidal irradiation (UVGI).
- Personal Protective Equipment (PPE): Respiratory protection, such as N95 respirators, for healthcare workers caring for TB patients, as well as appropriate use of gloves, gowns, and eye protection.

Contact Tracing and Screening

Identifying and screening individuals who have been in close contact with TB patients (contact tracing) is essential for early detection of TB infection and disease. Contact tracing involves:

- Interviewing TB Patients: Obtaining information about household contacts, close contacts at work or school, and other individuals who may have been exposed to TB.
- Tuberculin Skin Testing (TST) and Interferon-Gamma Release Assays (IGRAs): Screening close contacts for TB infection using TST or IGRA, followed by chest X-ray and microbiological testing if indicated.

Health Education Initiatives

Health education plays a critical role in raising awareness about TB transmission, symptoms, prevention, and treatment among healthcare providers, patients, and the general public. Key components of health education initiatives include:

Reduction: Addressing misconceptions and reducing stigma associated with TB, particularly among marginalized populations and individuals living with TB.

Global TB Control Strategies

The World Health Organization (WHO) has established global targets and strategies for TB prevention and control, including the End TB Strategy and the Sustainable Development Goals (SDGs). Key components of global TB control strategies include:

- Political Commitment: Mobilizing political leaders and policymakers to prioritize TB prevention, diagnosis, treatment, and research funding.
- Health System Strengthening: Building capacity within healthcare systems to deliver high-quality TB services, including diagnostics, treatment, and patient support.
- Research and Innovation: Investing in research and development for new TB diagnostics, drugs, and vaccines, as well as operational research to optimize TB care delivery.

Preventive measures and public health strategies are essential for controlling the spread of TB and reducing its global burden. By implementing vaccination programs, infection control measures, contact tracing, and health education initiatives, healthcare providers and public health officials can achieve significant progress towards eliminating TB as a public health threat.

DISCUSSION QUESTIONS

- What are the major barriers to effective TB management in low- and middle-income countries, and what strategies can be implemented to overcome these obstacles?
- Analyze the impact of stigma and discrimination on TB patients. How can healthcare providers and communities work to reduce these negative effects?

LESSON TWO: DIRECTIONS IN TB RESEARCH AND EDUCATION

The fight against TB continues to evolve with advancements in research, technology, and education. This lesson explores future directions in TB research and education, focusing on innovative approaches to diagnostics, treatment, vaccines, and public health strategies.

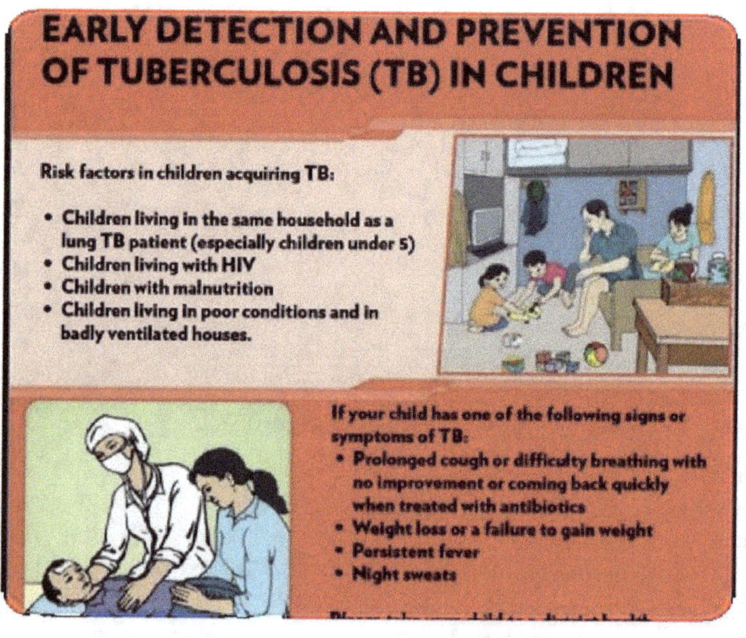

Advanced Diagnostics

Advances in diagnostic technologies are revolutionizing TB detection and monitoring. Emerging diagnostic tools include:

- Molecular Tests: Rapid molecular assays, such as nucleic acid amplification tests (NA

- Point-of-Care Testing: Expanding the availability and accuracy of point-of-care diagnostic tests to provide rapid, reliable results in resource-limited settings. Innovations like portable molecular testing devices and biosensors hold promise for decentralized TB testing.

- Biomarkers: Identifying and validating novel biomarkers for TB diagnosis, treatment monitoring, and prediction of disease progression. Biomarkers can enhance the sensitivity and specificity of current diagnostic tools and provide insights into host-pathogen interactions.
- Artificial Intelligence (AI) and Machine Learning: Leveraging AI and machine learning algorithms to analyze complex data from chest X-rays, CT scans, and molecular tests. These technologies can improve diagnostic accuracy, reduce interpretation time, and identify patterns indicative of drug resistance.

Innovative Treatments

Research into new TB treatments is critical to overcoming the challenges of drug resistance and lengthy treatment regimens. Promising areas of investigation include:

- New Drug Development: Discovering and developing new anti-TB drugs with novel mechanisms of action to combat drug-resistant TB strains. Potential candidates include bedaquiline, delamanid, and pretomanid, which target different bacterial processes.
- Shorter Treatment Regimens: Evaluating shorter, more effective treatment regimens to improve patient adherence and reduce the burden of prolonged therapy. Clinical trials are investigating combinations of new and existing drugs to achieve this goal.
- Host-Directed Therapies: Exploring therapies that modulate the host immune response to enhance the body's ability to fight TB infection. These therapies aim to reduce inflammation, improve bacterial clearance, and prevent tissue damage.

- Adjunctive Therapies: Investigating the use of adjunctive therapies, such as immunomodulators and anti-inflammatory agents, to complement standard TB treatment and improve patient outcomes.

Vaccine Development

Developing an effective TB vaccine is a top priority in global TB control efforts. Research focuses on:

- New Vaccine Candidates: Developing and testing new vaccine candidates, including subunit vaccines, viral vector vaccines, and live attenuated vaccines. These candidates aim to provide better protection against pulmonary TB in adults and children.
- Therapeutic Vaccines: Exploring vaccines designed to boost the immune response in individuals already infected with TB, helping to control or eliminate latent infection and prevent progression to active disease.
- Vaccine Delivery Systems: Innovating delivery systems, such as nanoparticle-based formulations and mucosal delivery routes, to enhance vaccine efficacy and immunogenicity.

Public Health Strategies

Future public health strategies aim to strengthen TB prevention, diagnosis, and treatment efforts worldwide. Key focus areas include:

- Integrated TB Care: Promoting integrated TB care within primary healthcare systems to improve access to comprehensive TB services, including diagnosis, treatment, and follow-up care.
- Digital Health Interventions: Implementing digital health tools, such as mobile apps, electronic health records, and telemedicine platforms, to enhance TB care delivery, patient monitoring, and treatment adherence.

- Community-Based Approaches: Strengthening community-based approaches to TB control, including engaging local leaders, training community health workers, and conducting outreach programs to raise awareness and support TB-affected individuals.
- Global Surveillance Networks: Expanding and enhancing global TB surveillance networks to monitor TB trends, track drug resistance patterns, and respond to emerging outbreaks.

Education and Training

Education and training are essential components of future TB control efforts. Priorities include:

- Healthcare Provider Training: Providing ongoing education and training for healthcare providers on the latest TB diagnostics, treatment protocols, and infection control measures. Training programs should emphasize multidisciplinary collaboration and patient-centered care.
- Public Awareness Campaigns: Conducting public awareness campaigns to educate communities about TB prevention, symptoms, and treatment. Campaigns should address stigma, promote early diagnosis, and encourage treatment adherence.
- Patient Education and Support: Developing educational materials and support resources for TB patients and their families to improve understanding of the disease, treatment regimens, and strategies for managing side effects and preventing transmission.
- Research Capacity Building: Investing in research capacity building in high TB burden countries to support local scientists and researchers in conducting TB research, developing innovative solutions, and contributing to global TB knowledge.

The future of TB research and education holds great promise for transforming TB prevention, diagnosis, treatment, and control. By embracing advanced diagnostics, innovative treatments, vaccine development, and comprehensive public health strategies, healthcare providers and researchers can make significant strides towards eliminating TB as a global health threat. Collaborative efforts, sustained funding, and a commitment to scientific excellence will be essential in achieving these goals and improving the lives of individuals affected by TB worldwide.

DISCUSSION QUESTIONS

- What are the promising areas of research in TB diagnostics, treatment, and prevention? How might these advances change the landscape of TB care in the next decade?
- Discuss the potential impact of new TB vaccines on global TB control efforts. What are the challenges and opportunities associated with developing and distributing these vaccines?

MODULE FIVE

LESSON ONE: TB TREATMENT MONITORING AND ADVERSE EFFECTS

Monitoring TB treatment is crucial for assessing response to therapy, ensuring medication adherence, and detecting adverse effects early. This lesson discusses the principles of treatment monitoring, common adverse effects of TB medications, and strategies for managing them.

Principles of Treatment Monitoring

Monitoring TB treatment involves assessing clinical response, microbiological tests, and adherence to medication regimens. Key components of treatment monitoring include:

- Clinical Assessment: Monitoring symptoms such as cough, fever, and weight loss to evaluate clinical improvement or deterioration.

- Microbiological Tests: Performing sputum smear microscopy, culture, and molecular tests to assess bacterial clearance and detect drug resistance.
- Radiographic Evaluation: Repeating chest X-rays or CT scans to evaluate changes in lung infiltrates, cavitation, and fibrosis.
- Laboratory Monitoring: Monitoring liver function tests to detect hepatotoxicity, as well as renal function and electrolytes in patients receiving certain TB medications.

Adverse Effects of TB Medications

TB medications can cause a range of adverse effects, which may vary in severity and onset. Common adverse effects include:

- Hepatotoxicity: Liver enzyme abnormalities and hepatitis due to medications such as isoniazid and rifampicin.
- Peripheral Neuropathy: Numbness, tingling, or pain in the extremities, often associated with isoniazid.
- Gastrointestinal Disturbances: Nausea, vomiting, and abdominal pain, particularly with rifampicin and pyrazinamide.
- Hypersensitivity Reactions: Skin rash, fever, and, rarely, severe allergic reactions to multiple TB medications.
- QT Interval Prolongation: Cardiac arrhythmias due to medications such as moxifloxacin, particularly in patients with pre-existing cardiac conditions.

Management of Adverse Effects

Managing adverse effects involves close monitoring, patient education, and, in some cases, modification of treatment regimens. Strategies for managing specific adverse effects include:

- Liver Function Monitoring: Regular monitoring of liver enzymes and clinical symptoms. Suspending hepatotoxic medications if severe abnormalities occur.

- Neuropathy Prevention: Supplementing pyridoxine (vitamin B6) to prevent peripheral neuropathy associated with isoniazid.
- Gastrointestinal Support: Administering antiemetics or adjusting medication schedules to minimize gastrointestinal disturbances.
- Allergy Management: Discontinuing offending medications and providing supportive care for hypersensitivity reactions.
- Cardiac Monitoring: Monitoring electrocardiograms (ECGs) and electrolytes in patients at risk of QT interval prolongation.

Patient Education and Counseling

Patient education is essential for promoting treatment adherence and early reporting of adverse effects. Healthcare providers should educate patients about:

- Potential Adverse Effects: Discussing common and serious adverse effects associated with TB medications.
- Monitoring Requirements: Explaining the need for regular clinical assessments, laboratory tests, and radiographic evaluations.
- Adherence Strategies: Providing strategies to improve medication adherence, such as pillboxes and reminder systems.
- Reporting Adverse Effects: Encouraging patients to report any new symptoms promptly to facilitate early intervention.

Monitoring TB treatment and managing adverse effects are integral components of successful TB management. By implementing systematic monitoring protocols, educating patients about potential adverse effects, and promptly addressing complications, healthcare providers can optimize treatment outcomes and improve patient safety.

DISCUSSION QUESTIONS

- How does TB diagnosis and treatment differ in pediatric populations compared to adults, and what specific challenges do healthcare providers face in managing TB in children?
- Discuss the implications of TB-HIV co-infection on treatment regimens and patient outcomes. What strategies can be implemented to manage both diseases effectively?

MODULE SIX

LESSON ONE: TB PREVENTION AND MANAGEMENT IN RESOURCE-LIMITED SETTINGS

TB remains a significant public health challenge in resource-limited settings, where socioeconomic factors, healthcare infrastructure, and access to diagnostic tools and medications can pose barriers to effective prevention and management. This lesson examines strategies to address TB in resource-limited settings, including innovative approaches, community engagement, and international collaborations.

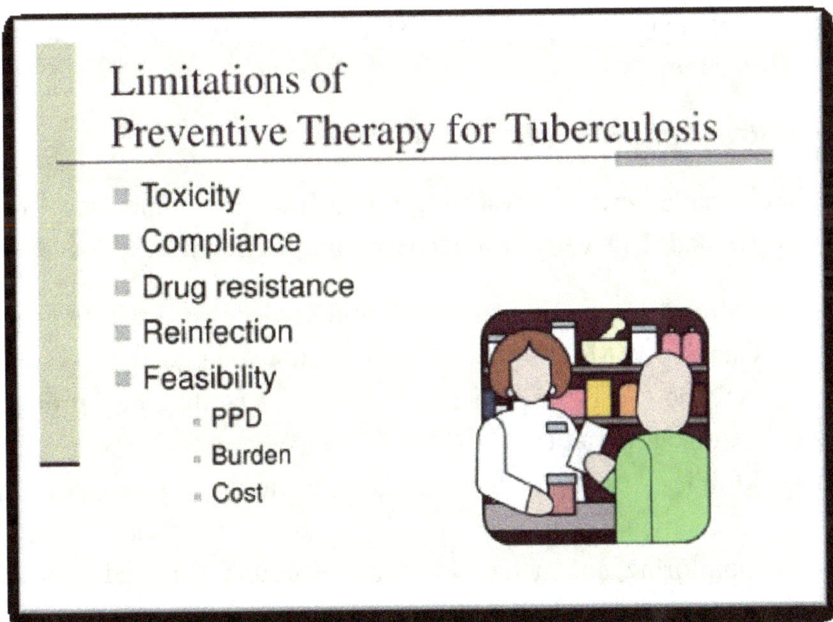

Challenges in Resource-Limited Settings

Resource-limited settings face numerous challenges in combating TB, including:

- Limited Access to Healthcare Services: Inadequate healthcare infrastructure, shortage of trained healthcare personnel, and geographical barriers can hinder TB diagnosis and treatment.
- Diagnostic Limitations: Limited access to reliable diagnostic tests, such as sputum smear microscopy, culture, and molecular assays, delays timely diagnosis and treatment initiation.
- Medication Shortages: Stockouts of essential TB medications, including first-line and second-line drugs, compromise treatment adherence and contribute to drug resistance.
- Socioeconomic Factors: Poverty, malnutrition, overcrowded living conditions, and lack of social support contribute to increased TB transmission and poor treatment outcomes.
- HIV Coinfection: High prevalence of HIV/AIDS complicates TB management, as HIV-infected individuals are at heightened risk of TB infection and progression to active disease.

Innovative Approaches to TB Control

Despite challenges, innovative approaches are improving TB prevention and management in resource-limited settings:

- Point-of-Care Diagnostics: Rapid molecular tests, such as GeneXpert MTB/RIF, provide same-day diagnosis of TB and detection of rifampicin resistance, facilitating prompt treatment initiation.
- Mobile Health Technologies: Mobile phones and telemedicine platforms enable remote consultation, patient monitoring, and medication adherence support in underserved areas.
- Community Health Workers: Trained community health workers play a vital role in TB case finding, treatment support, contact tracing, and health education within local communities.

- Integrated TB/HIV Services: Coordinated efforts to screen, diagnose, and treat TB and HIV/AIDS simultaneously improve outcomes and reduce mortality among coinfected individuals.

Community Engagement and Empowerment

Engaging communities in TB prevention and management efforts fosters ownership, promotes health literacy, and enhances treatment adherence. Strategies include:

- Community Education Programs: Raising awareness about TB transmission, symptoms, and treatment options through workshops, health fairs, and multimedia campaigns.
- Patient Support Groups: Establishing peer support networks and patient advocacy groups to empower individuals affected by TB and reduce stigma.
- Community-Based Treatment Support: Providing directly observed therapy (DOT) through community volunteers or family members to improve medication adherence and treatment outcomes.
- Collaborative Partnerships: Forming partnerships with local governments, non-governmental organizations (NGOs), and international agencies to mobilize resources and support sustainable TB control initiatives.

Global Initiatives and Funding Support

International collaborations and funding initiatives play a crucial role in advancing TB control efforts in resource-limited settings:

- Global Fund to Fight AIDS, Tuberculosis and Malaria: Providing financial support for TB programs, procurement of medications, and strengthening health systems in low-income countries.

- Stop TB Partnership: Facilitating partnerships between governments, donors, civil society, and healthcare providers to accelerate progress towards TB elimination goals.
- World Health Organization (WHO) Strategies: Implementing the End TB Strategy, Sustainable Development Goals (SDGs), and TB-Free Cities initiatives to reduce TB incidence and mortality globally.

Addressing TB in resource-limited settings requires a comprehensive approach that integrates innovative technologies, community engagement, and international collaborations. By overcoming diagnostic, treatment, and socioeconomic barriers, healthcare providers and stakeholders can achieve equitable access to TB prevention, diagnosis, and treatment services, ultimately reducing the global burden of TB.

DISCUSSION QUESTIONS

- What are the key components of a successful community health education campaign for TB prevention, and how can these campaigns be tailored to different cultural contexts?
- Discuss the role of community health workers in TB control. How can training and support for these workers be improved to enhance their effectiveness?

MODULE SEVEN

LESSON ONE: TB AND MULTIDRUG-RESISTANT TB (MDR-TB) MANAGEMENT

Managing multidrug-resistant TB (MDR-TB) poses significant challenges and requires specialized knowledge and approaches. This lesson delves into the complexities of MDR-TB, including diagnosis, treatment regimens, and the global efforts to combat this formidable public health threat.

MDR TB Control

- Extraordinary measures are needed in countries with the highest rates of TB and MDR TB: rapid detection, access to drugs and steady drugs supply and effective and expert care.

- The only reasonable approach is strengthening TB Control worldwide to prevent MDR TB and XDR TB

Understanding MDR-TB

MDR-TB is defined as TB that is resistant to at least isoniazid (INH) and rifampicin (RIF), the two most potent first-line anti-TB drugs. Factors contributing to the development of MDR-TB include inadequate treatment, non-adherence to treatment regimens, and transmission of resistant strains.

Diagnosis of MDR-TB

Accurate and timely diagnosis of MDR-TB is critical for effective management. Diagnostic approaches include:

- Molecular Tests: Rapid molecular tests such as GeneXpert MTB/RIF and line probe assays (LPAs) detect resistance to rifampicin and other first-line drugs, providing results within hours.
- Culture-Based Methods: Conventional culture and drug susceptibility testing (DST) on solid or liquid media remain the gold standard for diagnosing MDR-TB and guiding treatment, although they are time-consuming.
- Whole Genome Sequencing (WGS): WGS is an emerging tool that provides comprehensive information on drug resistance mutations, enabling precise tailoring of treatment regimens.

Treatment Regimens for MDR-TB

Treating MDR-TB involves longer, more complex regimens with second-line drugs. Key components of MDR-TB treatment include:

- Standardized Regimens: WHO-recommended standardized regimens for MDR-TB typically include a combination of second-line injectable agents (such as kanamycin, amikacin, or capreomycin) and fluoroquinolones (such as levofloxacin or moxifloxacin), along with other drugs like ethionamide, cycloserine, and para-aminosalicylic acid.
- Individualized Regimens: Tailoring treatment based on individual drug susceptibility results is crucial for optimizing outcomes. Newer drugs like bedaquiline and delamanid are reserved for patients with extensively drug-resistant TB (XDR-TB) or those who cannot tolerate standard regimens.
- Shorter Regimens: Recent research has supported the use of shorter, all-oral regimens for MDR-TB, typically lasting 9-12

months, compared to the traditional 18-24 months. These regimens improve adherence and reduce treatment burden.

Adverse Effects and Monitoring

Second-line TB drugs often cause significant adverse effects, requiring careful monitoring and management. Common adverse effects include:

- Nephrotoxicity and Ototoxicity: Associated with injectable agents like kanamycin and amikacin.
- Psychiatric Symptoms: Depression, psychosis, and suicidal ideation, particularly with cycloserine.
- Electrolyte Imbalances: Hypokalemia and hypomagnesemia due to medications like capreomycin.
- Peripheral Neuropathy: Numbness and tingling from drugs such as linezolid and fluoroquinolones.

Global Efforts to Combat MDR-TB

- Global initiatives and collaborations are essential for addressing the MDR-TB crisis:
- Green Light Committee (GLC): Supports countries in implementing WHO-recommended MDR-TB management programs and ensuring access to quality-assured second-line drugs.
- TB REACH: Provides funding and technical support for innovative approaches to TB case finding and treatment, including MDR-TB.
- Global Fund and UNITAID: Provide financial resources to scale up MDR-TB programs and improve access to diagnostics and treatments in high-burden countries.

MDR-TB management requires a multifaceted approach that includes advanced diagnostics, individualized treatment regimens, and robust global support. By staying informed about the latest developments and adhering to best practices, healthcare providers can improve outcomes for patients with MDR-TB and contribute to global efforts to eliminate TB.

DISCUSSION QUESTIONS

- How can the development of rapid, point-of-care diagnostic tests transform TB detection and treatment in resource-limited settings?
- Discuss the potential impact of new TB vaccines currently in development. What are the main challenges in bringing these vaccines to market and ensuring their widespread use?

CONCLUSION

In conclusion, the path to TB eradication is complex and requires sustained efforts across multiple fronts. Healthcare providers, policymakers, researchers, and communities must work together to implement effective strategies, overcome barriers, and adapt to evolving challenges. By embracing innovation, fostering collaboration, and committing to comprehensive TB control measures, we can make significant strides towards a world free of tuberculosis. This eBook serves as a valuable resource for healthcare providers, offering in-depth knowledge and practical guidance to enhance their role in combating this pervasive disease. In conclusion, the path to TB eradication is complex and requires sustained efforts across multiple fronts. Healthcare providers, policymakers, researchers, and communities must work together to implement effective strategies, overcome barriers, and adapt to evolving challenges. By embracing innovation, fostering collaboration, and committing to comprehensive TB control measures, we can make significant strides towards a world free of tuberculosis. This eBook serves as a valuable resource for healthcare providers, offering in-depth knowledge and practical guidance to enhance their role in combating this pervasive disease. In conclusion, the path to TB eradication is complex and requires sustained efforts across multiple fronts. Healthcare providers, policymakers, researchers, and communities must work together to implement effective strategies, overcome barriers, and adapt to evolving challenges. By embracing innovation, fostering collaboration, and committing to comprehensive TB control measures, we can make significant strides towards a world free of tuberculosis. This eBook serves as a valuable resource for healthcare providers, offering in-depth knowledge and practical guidance to enhance their role in combating this pervasive disease.

REFERENCES

- Bloom, B. R., & Murray, C. J. (1992). *Tuberculosis: Commentary on a reemergent killer. Science,* 257(5073)
- Centers for Disease Control and Prevention. (2016*). Tuberculosis (TB): Diagnosis and treatment.*
- Cohen, A., Mathiasen, V. D., Schön, T., & Wejse, C. (2019). The global prevalence of latent tuberculosis: a systematic review and meta-analysis. European Respiratory Journal, 54(3).
- Dheda, K., Barry, C. E., & Maartens, G. (2016). *Tuberculosis. Th, e Lancet*387(10024)
- Frieden, T. R., Sterling, T. R., Munsiff, S. S., Watt, C. J., & Dye, C. (2003). *Tuberculosis. The Lancet,* 362(9387).
- Gandhi, N. R., Nunn, P., Dheda, K., Schaaf, H. S., Zignol, M., van Soolingen, D., Jensen, P., & Bayona, J. (2010). *Multidrug-resistant and extensively drug-resistant tuberculosis: a threat to global control of tuberculosis. The Lancet,* 375(9728),
- Getahun, H., Matteelli, A., Abubakar, I., Aziz, M. A., Baddeley, A., Barreira, D., ... & Raviglione, M. (2015*). Management of latent Mycobacterium tuberculosis infection: WHO guidelines for low tuberculosis burden countries. European Respiratory Journal,* 46(6)
- Lönnroth, K., Jaramillo, E., Williams, B. G., Dye, C., & Raviglione, M. (2009). *Drivers of tuberculosis epidemics: the role of risk factors and social determinants. Social Science & Medicine,* 68(12).